# Contents

# Preface

In October 1998 Scottish CCC – now Learning and Teaching Scotland – began an extensive consultation exercise following a Ministerial request to review the 1993 Guidelines for Environmental Studies 5–14. Primary and secondary schools, teacher education institutions, local authorities, professional associations and relevant interest groups were all given the opportunity to participate both in a preliminary consultation and in the later consultation on the draft revised guidelines. The aim of the review was to help teachers implement the guidelines by making them clearer and more manageable and to enhance pupil attainment. It was therefore decided to remove the ICT and health education components from environmental studies and to issue separate guidelines for these two important aspects of the 5–14 curriculum.

As a consequence of removing ICT from environmental studies the guidelines differ to a greater extent than other revised guidelines. These guidelines therefore replace the Information Technology (IT) component of the environmental studies 5–14 guidelines issued in March 1993. The decision to publish guidelines for information and communications technology (ICT) reflects a widespread view that its importance across all aspects of the curriculum is such that it merits a separate coherent curriculum framework.

Although the structure of these ICT guidelines is not obviously similar to the IT component of the environmental studies 5–14 guidelines of 1993, it does reflect changes in technology and ICT practices in schools. Much of the content, however, is familiar and schools should be well placed to begin relating existing provision in ICT to the new framework.

These guidelines are set within the context of other 5–14 developments: other national guidelines also contain advice on the contribution of ICT within specific curriculum areas. They provide a revised structure of strands and attainment targets on which schools can plan effective ICT provision.

In the world at large, it is acknowledged that ICT is growing at a rapid pace, with emerging technologies continuing to develop. The impact on education has been fairly significant but is likely to increase more dramatically over the next few years as schools develop greater ICT capability. This will happen through an increase in the numbers of computers in schools, connection through local and wide area networks and the development of teachers' awareness and skills in ICT. The pace of change in ICT means that an ongoing programme of support will be required, and that the curriculum guidance contained in these guidelines will require review and updating as a matter of routine practice. ICT itself will prove to be a valuable tool to assist in this.

These guidelines are commended to all concerned with the education of pupils aged 5–14.

Mike Baughan
Chief Executive, Learning and Teaching Scotland

# Introduction

This document sets out guidelines for the development of information and communications technology (ICT) capability for pupils aged 5–14 in Scottish schools at the beginning of the twenty-first century.

The guidelines are based on existing good practice, but also take account of local initiatives and the national development agenda. They set out a progression of knowledge, skills and attitudes in ICT as pupils progress through primary school and the first two years of secondary school.

The guidelines set out a *rationale*, its associated aim and *framework* for the progression of knowledge, skills and attitudes in ICT 5–14. They describe content and contexts for pupils' learning. This requires careful *planning and managing*. Broad advice on *learning, teaching and assessing* is also included to assist schools ensure effective, progressive development of pupils' ICT capability.

The guidelines describe a single *attainment outcome* and series of *strands and targets* for appropriate progression through the levels of concepts and skills in ICT, which generally build on those developed earlier.

It is not expected that all of ICT 5–14 will be introduced at once. Time will be needed for implementation of a range of issues, such as the development of pupil outcomes at one level so that they can be built upon during the next. Schools and teachers are encouraged to regard the implementation of ICT 5–14 as a developmental process and not as a single event. The start of this process is familiarisation by all staff with the guidelines, then a review of existing practice and agreement on an action plan for development. The *Guide for Teachers and Managers* develops these ideas further.

The guidelines are designed to provide a framework for the integration of ICT into existing classroom practice so that all pupils become skilled, confident and informed users and also gain the maximum benefit in using ICT in other curricular areas. These guidelines promote the permeation of *ICT across the other curriculum areas of 5–14*.

There follows an example of how ICT can be integrated within, and used to enrich, other 5–14 curriculum areas, and further examples are provided in Section 6 of this document.

A class of Primary 5–7 pupils undertook a project on road safety. Part of the project considered the issue of wearing seat belts in the back of a car. A survey of staff and members of the local community who drive cars provided the pupils with enough data to produce a chart of their findings. Comparative information and statistics on national surveys were acquired from the Department of the Environment's website: *Belt Up in the Back. For Everyone's Sake.*

**Curriculum areas:** environmental studies, health education

**ICT strands:** *collecting and analysing information, searching and researching*

This example gives a flavour of how ICT can be, and currently is, set in context and can contribute to the 5–14 curriculum.

These guidelines conclude with reference to *specific issues* for ICT such as the articulation of 5–14 with other stages of learning, the importance of ICT as a core skill, and a number of important current national initiatives that recognise and support the development of ICT.

Section 1

# Rationale

## What is ICT and why is it important?

Information and communications technology (ICT) is generally regarded as the overlap of computer information and telecommunications technologies, and their applications. In this document the term ICT is used to indicate the whole range of technologies involved in information processing and electronic communications, including the internet, electronic mail and videoconferencing.

In recent years ICT has had, and is continuing to have, an increasingly significant impact on all aspects of society. There are few areas of life, at home and in work, where this new technology has not made an impact. ICT expands our access to, and understanding of, the world at large. It allows people in all areas life to benefit from the power of computers as a personal tool, to collaborate in groups and to communicate locally and globally.

The importance of ICT cannot be overestimated. Young people in our schools today will require considerable ICT knowledge, skills and awareness if they are to be successful in their futures, and the economy will depend on a high level of ICT capability from its people if it is to develop technologically and to compete internationally.

As well as the need to develop ICT knowledge and skills for both individuals and society at large, ICT also offers the education process one of the most potentially powerful learning tools available. Not only can computers support learning across the whole curriculum, but communication networks also provide the learner with fast and searchable access to vast amounts of information. In addition to this, ICT supports a wide range of broader educational objectives including independent learning, collaboration with others and communication skills.

It is thus of vital importance that all young people have adequate access to ICT and that they develop the necessary skills, taking full advantage of the learning capabilities that ICT offers. Schools have a special responsibility to ensure that young people receive the provision that they are entitled to. As the 5–14 stages represent 9 out of the 11 years of compulsory education, they have a key role to play in developing ICT capability.

Several aspects of ICT are particularly significant for schools. These are:
- the importance of developing ICT skills to meet the needs of the individual and society
- exploiting the potential of ICT to support learning and teaching across the curriculum
- the uses of ICT to support broader educational aims, such as positive dispositions towards learning, enhanced presentation of work, problem solving and investigative approaches
- the potential for communicating and researching locally and globally, including access to a global bank of information
- the ability to share ideas and work collaboratively
- the ability to access expertise through a variety of techniques.

Ultimately the educational purpose of ICT should be to assist pupils to play their full part in society. They should be well informed about the current and potential applications of ICT and be skilled and effective in using them. They must be able to evaluate the effectiveness of the resources provided by ICT and determine when it is most appropriate to use them.

Growing out of such a rationale, these guidelines provide advice to assist teachers to develop ICT capability fully in young people and to realise the potential of ICT as a teaching and learning tool. The resulting experiences of ICT for pupils will ensure that they are equipped with ICT knowledge, skills and attitudes that they can apply across the curriculum and use to develop their understanding of the world at large.

These guidelines have identified the importance of ICT to the individual pupil, the contribution ICT can make to the development of other curricular areas and to learning in general. They have also clearly identified the impact of ICT on future prosperity in a knowledge-based economy. The overall aim of ICT 5–14 must, however, relate to the development of the knowledge, skills and informed attitudes of individual pupils; thus the aim is:

- *to develop in young people knowledge, skills and informed attitudes in relation to information and communications technology.*

A number of objectives derive from this broad statement of aim. ICT in 5–14 will encourage pupils to:

- develop confidence and skills in using ICT
- make use of ICT to create and present their own ideas and material
- use ICT to collect and analyse structured information and to solve problems
- employ ICT to search for information and to research topics
- use ICT to communicate and collaborate with others
- employ ICT to control and model aspects of the environment
- be aware of and be informed about the applications and implications of ICT in society.

The aim and objectives lead directly to the attainment outcome and strands within ICT 5–14.

Section 2

# Framework for ICT

## The attainment outcome, strands and targets

### Attainment outcome

Effective understanding and use of ICT involves the development of knowledge, skills and attitudes. Knowledge develops alongside skills. Attitudes can be meaningful only in relation to skills, knowledge and contexts that have previously been developed. Programmes of work and pupil activities develop all three elements together. For these reasons, the single attainment outcome for ICT 5–14 relating directly to the overall stated aim is *developing ICT capability*.

### Strands

Just as the attainment outcome of ICT 5–14 relates directly to the overall stated aim, the strands emerge directly from the specific objectives. The strands of ICT 5–14 are:

* *using the technology*, which is concerned with the building of knowledge and understanding of the technology and the development of skills and confidence in using the technology effectively and responsibly
* *creating and presenting*, which involves the development of the ICT knowledge and skills that pupils will need to create and effectively present their own ideas and other material
* *collecting and analysing*, which deals with the use of ICT tools to collect and analyse structured information, such as databases and spreadsheets, and to solve problems
* *searching and researching*, which addresses the development of skills and concepts in using ICT to search for information and to research topics. It involves the effective use of resources such as CD-ROMs and the internet
* *communicating and collaborating*, which is concerned with the use of ICT to communicate and collaborate with other individuals and groups. It involves the appropriate use of tools and techniques, such as e-mail and conferencing, as well as comparisons with traditional communication methods
* *controlling and modelling*, which involves the development of knowledge and skills in using computers to instruct and control devices as well as to take measurements of, and model, the environment
* *developing informed attitudes in relation to ICT in society*. In this strand pupils progressively develop informed attitudes about the applications and implications of ICT in society.

### Attainment targets A–F

In the wider 5–14 programme there are specific attainment targets within each strand. These provide clear statements of what pupils should know and be able to do at each of the levels A to F. These six levels are common to the 5–14 programme and are based on the following descriptions.

Level A:    should be attainable in the course of P1–P3 by almost all pupils.
Level B:    should be attainable by some pupils in P3 or even earlier, but certainly by most in P4.
Level C:    should be attainable in the course of P4–P6 by most pupils.
Level D:    should be attainable by some pupils in P5–P6 or even earlier, but certainly by most in P7.

Level E:   should be attainable by some pupils in P7–S1, but certainly by most in S2.

Level F:   should be attainable in part by some pupils, and completed by a few pupils, in the course of P7–S2.

The strands and the associated attainment targets for ICT are further developed in Section 5: Attainment Outcome, Strands and Targets.

**It is important to recognise that this framework is a way of describing the curriculum and of identifying the desired outcomes of learning in ICT; it does not prescribe a particular approach to teaching.**

# Planning and Managing ICT

## 3.1 Planning and managing

The central principles of the 5–14 programme are balance, breadth, coherence, continuity and progression. In planning and managing ICT, schools should ensure that pupils are provided with:

- *broad and balanced* learning opportunities within ICT skills and applications across the 5–14 curriculum
- *coherent* links and connections
- *continuous* pathways for learning
- *progressive* development of understanding, skills and informed attitudes in relation to ICT.

Planning for ICT in schools can usefully be viewed as operating on two parallel tracks. Necessary longer-term strategic/development planning will take place at authority and school management levels and be developed across stages, departments and within clusters of associated schools. Alongside this there is also the classroom teachers' short-term planning that draws on the strategic overview for specific ICT activities, units of work or topics.

Schools work in partnership with their local authority, which has the responsibility to ensure ICT provision including resources, training and support, and to policies and practices dealing with a range of issues such as safe uses of the internet. In meeting these requirements, local authorities have adopted differing models of ICT service provision, including services direct to schools or supplying managed services in partnership with an external provider.

In the *Guide for Teachers and Managers*, more detailed advice is given. This includes commentary appropriate to local authorities, followed by advice on whole-school and individual classroom issues.

Management responsibilities at these three levels have distinctive features but also a number of common elements.

- Provision of effective implementation strategies and leadership, including thorough planning and the definition of the roles and responsibilities of all involved.
- Definition of the place of ICT within the existing curriculum, including the expectations of attainment, the quality of learning and teaching sought and the importance of continuity and progression, assessment and monitoring.
- Review of resources including staffing, provision of hardware and software, accommodation and infrastructure needs.
- Audit of staff development needs and planning an appropriate programme.
- Setting clear expectations of pupil attainment, and establishing strategies for monitoring and evaluating these.
- Communication with parents and the wider community to secure involvement and active partnership.

### 3.2 Managing assessment

The permeation model for ICT 5–14 requires that schools have a clear policy for coordinating ICT provision for pupils. Teachers need to know which aspects of ICT 5–14 they are to deliver at a particular stage and in a given curricular area, their responsibilities for assessment and how to record pupils' progress so that the information can usefully be used by others. Teachers need to plan for pupils' progressive development in ICT as well as the use of ICT in teaching and learning.

Successful planning for the progressive development of ICT skills must ensure that time is found to:

- teach new concepts and skills
- practise and reinforce concepts and skills
- meet individuals' developmental needs
- assess progress and attainment in ICT.

To plan successfully for the use of ICT in learning and teaching, teachers need to know the prior learning that can be assumed within a class, group or individual pupil.

Issues of assessment in the progressive development of pupils' skills are also discussed in Section 4 of this document, in the *Guide for Teachers and Managers* and in other documents to be published nationally.

# Teaching, Learning and Assessing ICT

## 4.1 Teaching and learning

Although ICT 5–14 has the single attainment outcome *developing ICT capability*, programmes of study in other curricular areas provide ideal opportunities for the development in pupils of other important educational outcomes. In learning about ICT and using it across the curriculum, pupils will be able to harness the potential of ICT to demonstrate creativity, enterprising activity and innovation. Challenges posed by ICT and the resulting sense of achievement stimulate pupils and can significantly contribute to the educational process by developing:

* communication and language skills
* presentation skills
* analytical and problem solving skills
* mathematical skills
* skills in self-directed learning and personal research
* skills in effective collaboration with others
* skills in critical evaluation and making informed judgements
* a sense of social and environmental responsibility
* learning skills for personal development.

These guidelines do not set out particular approaches or methods in teaching and learning ICT. Effective learning and teaching in ICT begins with planning and will take account of a number of other issues described in these guidelines, including pupils' interests, previous experiences and attainments. The attainment outcome *developing ICT capability* and its associated strands and targets is a framework within which teachers and schools will plan teaching and learning flexibly. Many activities in ICT involve pupils in moving in and around strands and specific targets. It is important that teachers are clear about what is being tackled in ICT activities and how effective planning ensures coverage. A number of classroom examples of ICT in teaching and learning are provided in Section 6.

In developing pupils' ICT capability, the quality of interaction between teacher and pupils is fundamental.

Characteristics of effective teaching and learning in ICT include:

* the quality of the teaching process
* the quality of pupils learning
* meeting pupils' needs.

## 4.2 Quality of the teaching process

Teachers have to allocate time to teach and consolidate ICT capability. In a successful session involving ICT the teacher will:

* be well prepared and have included planned structured activities
* have identified clear and appropriate objectives for ICT skills and/or curricular aspects and have included steps to ensure equality of opportunity
* use a variety of strategies to stimulate pupils

- ensure appropriate use of relevant technical vocabulary
- take due account of what pupils are learning at home or outwith the classroom setting generally to develop their ICT capability.

## 4.3 Quality of pupils' learning

In a successful session involving ICT, pupils are:

- motivated, challenged and required to think for themselves
- encouraged to be independent and confident users of technology
- set tasks that encourage cooperation and collaboration and to solve given problems.

## 4.4 Meeting pupils' needs

In a successful session involving ICT teachers will:

- provide appropriate challenges to all pupils based on their prior attainment
- provide variety, including good use of available technology
- assist pupils' learning by making connections with other areas of the curriculum in meaningful ways
- make good use of appropriate specialist and other support staff, such as classroom assistants or school librarians, to facilitate learning.

In considering how to ensure appropriate pace and challenge, teachers should take account of the following aspects of progression in ICT.

- The development of ICT skills will move from 'supported' to 'independent'.
- Pre-defined structures will progress into the requirement for pupils to create their own.
- Working confidently with single media (for example text) will progress to multimedia (text/ sound/graphics).
- Single-solution problems will progress to those with a choice of solutions.
- Simple searching will progress to more refined searches and critical evaluation.
- Increasing knowledge of the applications of ICT in society will lead to the development of informed views on their implications.
- Competent use of the technology will progress to informed and responsible use.

Progression can also be described as a gradual move from exposure to specific ICT situations, through the processes of acquiring basic skills to the eventual competence gained by consolidation, and on to more advanced and creative uses of ICT.

These ideas should be helpful to teachers in their planning for pupils' progression and next steps in learning.

These issues are discussed in greater detail in the *Guide for Teachers and Managers*.

## 4.5 Assessing in 5–14

The *National Guidelines: Assessment 5–14* should be the first reference point for advice on the assessment of attainment in ICT. The guidelines set assessment and recording in the context of effective learning and teaching, suggesting that the process of assessment includes attention to five key activities: planning, teaching, recording, reporting and evaluating.

The rationale for the place of ICT across 5–14 has been described in this document, along with the attainment outcome, strands and attainment targets. These are further exemplified in the *Guide for Teachers and Managers* to help teachers establish clear contexts and objectives for learning and teaching and to assess pupils' progress in relation to these objectives.

## 4.6 Assessing ICT

The ICT focus for assessment as a part of teaching will be familiar in the context of established performance indicators. This involves teachers being clear about the ICT entitlement for pupils at their stage(s); and about the need for a succinct and useful record of pupils' strengths and development needs in each strand and the need to use this to inform the planning process.

Effective assessment in ICT is well matched to curricular targets and can be formal as well as informal, written as well as practical.

In ICT 5–14 pupils will learn:

- practical skills in using computer hardware, software and communications technologies
- knowledge and understanding about ICT
- the development of informed attitudes about the uses of computers in society.

Contexts for assessing these might derive naturally from the use of ICT in learning and teaching. Sometimes contexts might have to be created specifically. It may be that acquisition of knowledge and understanding can be demonstrated by the completion of certain practical ICT-focused tasks. Alternatively, it may be appropriate to assess knowledge and understanding of an aspect of ICT separately through an oral or written task. The same could apply to the development of informed attitudes. Assessments will typically comprise practical, oral and written work or a mixture of all three.

Further guidance on planning and managing the assessment process is given in Section 3.

## 4.7 Means of assessment

Evidence of progress and attainment in ICT is found in the accepted pattern of what pupils say, write and do. It comes from the teacher's:

- observation of, and discussions with, pupils
- examination of pupils' written work
- examination of hard-copy output.

A particular predefined task may provide evidence for assessment of learning objectives for a single strand within ICT, or for assessment across strands. For example, the production of a report followed by a talk to classmates about the main report findings could involve pupils in:

- *using the technology* appropriately
- *creating and presenting* to prepare the report and the presentation
- *searching and researching* to obtain the relevant information.

Alternatively, from time to time, assessments could focus on a specific strand or an aspect of a strand.

Pupils' progress and attainment in aspects of ICT will often be obvious to teachers through the pupils' repeated demonstration of their knowledge, understanding and skills in various curriculum areas. Teachers might also set pupils specific assessment tasks to complete. It will be important for the teacher to judge carefully when to observe from a distance and when to interact with a pupil as part of the assessment process. Often pupils will be working in pairs or in small groups. Talking with pupils and asking them questions about what they are doing, or what they have produced, as part of an assessment task will allow the pupils to articulate their thinking and demonstrate their understanding. Having identified a focus for assessment, teachers can then:

- watch pupils as they plan and carry out activities
- listen to pupils as they talk to each other
- talk with pupils and ask them questions
- make judgements about products of pupils' work as evidence of learning.

In assessing ICT it will often be important to share with pupils the criteria, based on the appropriate attainment targets, against which the pupils' work is to be judged. Criteria shared with pupils can also form a useful basis for self- and peer-assessment, where this is part of a school's assessment procedures.

## 4.8 Recording

Schools have to use ICT flexibility according to their resources, experience, expertise and their aspirations for their pupils, while ensuring that pupils make appropriate progress in ICT. It is unlikely that pupils will experience ICT and develop ICT capability strand by strand and level by level precisely as set out in these guidelines. Schools need to be clear about their expectations of pupils' progress and attainments at each stage and be in a position to record the achievements of the class, groups and individuals, as appropriate. To achieve this, schools will need to adapt the framework for ICT 5–14 to suit their circumstances. Collaboration will be needed so that ICT attainment information can be effectively shared as pupils move from primary to secondary school.

Technology increasingly has potential as an efficient recording tool to facilitate information flow about progress and attainment in ICT, and for this information to be analysed and shared, especially in secondary schools where a number of teachers and departments are responsible for ICT provision.

## 4.9 Reporting

Schools should be in a position to explain succinctly to parents how the 5–14 ICT framework operates in their school. Reporting on pupils' attainment should contain detail on specific strands as appropriate.

Section 5

# Attainment Outcome, Strands and Targets

A familiar 5–14 model of an *attainment outcome* with a number of *strands and targets*, in this case related to the ICT aspect of the curriculum, is introduced in Section 2: Framework for ICT.

The single *attainment outcome* described for ICT, *developing ICT capability*, involves the development of knowledge, skills and attitudes.

The *strands* of ICT 5–14 are:

* *using the technology*
* *creating and presenting*
* *collecting and analysing*
* *searching and researching*
* *communicating and collaborating*
* *controlling and modelling*
* *developing informed attitudes in relation to ICT in society.*

The *attainment targets* within each *strand* provide clear statements of what pupils should know and be able to do at each of the levels A–F.

The grid that follows provides schools with a model of attainment targets for the attainment outcome and for each of its strands at each level A–F, and provides pupils with a coherent learning entitlement in ICT.

The major purpose of this grid is to provide teachers with a common framework in planning for effective learning, in monitoring pupil progress and experiences, and in assessing, recording and reporting.

In addition, as has already been stated, the nature of learning in ICT often involves pupils moving naturally around targets or levels within a strand, or among several different strands within the overall framework.

Some strands and their associated targets may be met through planned separate provision for ICT skills development, and others through the contextualised application of ICT in other 5–14 curriculum areas. This distinction is important but not clear-cut and schools will use their judgement in planning a variety of approaches to be used. Again, careful planning and managing is required to ensure consistency of provision.

The framework of strands and targets should be viewed as providing a number of important reference points, or milestones of achievement, that ensure coverage over time, and not as a prescriptive programme of study or linear series of activities and experiences.

It is important to recognise that this framework describes key skills in ICT that can be used in a number of curricular contexts; it does not prescribe particular approaches that schools will adopt to the arrangements for the teaching of ICT within 5–14.

Detailed exemplification of how schools might elaborate the strands is found in the *Guide for Teachers and Managers*. This level of detail and specification will support teachers in understanding the expected pupil attainments and in planning ICT 5–14.

# Developing ICT capability – strands and attainment targets

**Pupils are able to:**

| Strand | Level A | Level B | Level C |
|---|---|---|---|
| **Using the technology** | • use a mouse to point and click<br>• start up/shut down the computer<br>• use a keyboard/concept keyboard<br>• print by clicking a 'print' button<br>• save and retrieve work, with support | • use menus and further mouse controls<br>• start and close an application; create a new document<br>• know the use of 'username' and 'password'<br>• save and retrieve work independently | • use the components of a 'windows' environment<br>• use a computer securely and responsibly<br>• use a computer on a network<br>• use another input device |
| **Creating and presenting:**<br><br>– text | • create, enter and amend one or more sentences without teacher support | • create and edit a piece of text, e.g. menu, invitation, story, and print out work | • create and edit a document, e.g. report, newspaper article, letter, using increasingly extended text-handling features |
| – graphics | • create a picture using simple software | • create a document with text and graphics using simple software | • create a document with text and graphics using more sophisticated software |
| – multimedia | • add text to a picture | • create a multimedia page using simple software | • create a simple multimedia presentation, e.g. slide show/web page using appropriate software |
| **Collecting and analysing** | • use non-computer databases<br>• use simple predefined computer databases | • enter data into a predefined database<br>• browse records and produce a simple report with support | • understand the structure of a database<br>• interrogate a database<br>• create a simple database<br>• produce reports independently |
| **Searching and researching** | • recognise that information is available electronically | • access information on CD-ROM with support<br>• access websites with pre-set bookmarks | • use teletext<br>• access CD-ROMs independently<br>• use a web browser independently<br>• print selectively |
| **Communicating and collaborating** | • show awareness that messages can be communicated electronically<br>• give simple comparisons with telephone/post | • make simple person-to-person communication, e.g. e-mail<br>• describe simple comparisons between phone/fax/e-mail | • manage their own electronic communications, e.g. managing a mailbox<br>• show an awareness of the style of communication (genre)<br>• be aware of, and describe, issues surrounding responsible use |
| **Controlling and modelling** | • follow directional instructions. | • control a screen image through simple instructions, e.g. a turtle<br>• use simple simulation/ adventure games. | • control an external device by giving instructions in single steps, e.g. floor turtle/robot arm<br>• use more complex simulation/ adventure games requiring a higher level of decision making. |
| **Developing informed attitudes** | As pupils progress through levels A–F they increasingly:<br>• recognise and appreciate the role of ICT in accessing information and knowledge, fostering creativity and facilitating the exchange of ideas<br>• appreciate the personal and societal benefits of ICT | | |

| Level D | Level E | Level F |
|---------|---------|---------|
| • use help facilities<br>• understand that there are different types of computer<br>• understand the need for backing up files and be able to do so<br>• understand the advantage of being able to share files | • interpret simple computer specifications such as speed and memory<br>• understand the costs of accessing network services<br>• use other peripherals as appropriate | • use manuals and on-line help to resolve simple hardware and software problems<br>• understand how a computer and its peripherals and software work together in simple terms |
| • create and edit a document, e.g. card, calendar, school newspaper, using more advanced text-handling features<br><br>• create a document, e.g. magazine, advert, using a range of drawing/painting facilities<br><br>• create a more sophisticated slide show/presentation or web pages with teacher support | • create a document incorporating textual, graphical and statistical information<br><br>• create a document using and manipulating a wide range of graphic material<br><br>• create a multimedia presentation or web pages working independently | • create a document using a desktop publishing software package<br><br>• produce a well-presented document incorporating a high level of graphics manipulation<br><br>• create a multimedia presentation or web pages incorporating a wide range of multimedia features |
| • use database reports including searching and sorting<br>• understand the structure of a spreadsheet<br>• enter data into a spreadsheet | • analyse problems, implement and evaluate solutions using database and spreadsheet<br>• model simple scenarios using spreadsheet<br>• produce graphs | • compare databases and spreadsheets as solutions to problems<br>• use more advanced functions of databases and spreadsheets |
| • search across a range of media<br>• use a search engine<br>• create bookmarks<br>• capture text and graphics by copying and pasting | • apply web searches to real-life situations<br>• download files<br>• refine searches<br>• compare two websites | • use specialist search engines<br>• refine searches using logical operators<br>• make critical evaluation of websites and search engines |
| • carry out simple shared activity, e.g. group communication/collaboration by e-mail<br>• demonstrate integration of e-mail with other software attachments<br>• show awareness of advantages/misuse of appropriate styles/genres | • take part in group collaboration activity, e.g. electronic conference<br>• show awareness of appropriate style and etiquette of conferencing | • instigate/manage a group activity, e.g. electronic forum/conference<br>• understand and use different collaborative approaches, e.g. real-time/without time constraints |
| • plan a sequence of instructions to be executed by a device<br>• be aware that computers can collect information about the environment through sensors, e.g. temperature, light, sound<br>• be aware that computers can be used to simulate/model real situations and be aware why they are used for this purpose, e.g. hazardous situations/training. | • control a device through a more complex sequence of instructions, e.g. ones containing a loop<br>• use a computer to collect and process data from the environment. | • create a set of computer instructions to solve a problem<br>• select appropriate input and output devices to solve problems. |

• become aware of the implications of the uses of ICT in different situations, e.g. the workplace, the home
• appreciate the need for responsible use of ICT and the need to protect information, individuals and society from its misuse
• appreciate when it is and is not appropriate to use ICT.

Section 6

# ICT Across the 5–14 Curriculum

## ICT in relation to other 5–14 curriculum areas

Developing pupils' ICT capability provides them with a range of knowledge, skills and attitudes applicable across the 5–14 curriculum. Since ICT permeates the 5–14 curriculum it performs the dual role of developing ICT skills in context, while at the same time using ICT capability to contribute to learning within other 5–14 curriculum areas. The examples of classroom practice given here show the range of ICT applications and how they enrich learning across the curriculum.

Whilst engaged in a class project on World War II, pupils in a P7 class searched the internet for information on related topics of their own choice, for example 'Aircraft' or 'The D-Day landings'. They selected appropriate material and used the information, pictures and sound clips they collected to create their own slide shows, which they then presented to other pupils.

**Curriculum area:**
environmental studies

**ICT strands:**
*searching and researching*, *creating and presenting*

The introduction of ICT has proved to be potentially very effective in supporting group and individual work and in facilitating the creation of a much greater variety of stimulating and challenging tasks across the curriculum.

All seven strands of ICT 5–14 described earlier have the potential to make significant contributions in each of the curricular areas of the 5–14 programme. There are a number of 5–14 curricular areas that have recently been reviewed, resulting in revised national guidelines being issued. Teachers should refer to the ICT advice in these other guidelines for more detailed ICT guidance related to that curricular area.

For example in *Environmental Studies – Society, Science and Technology: National Guidelines 5–14* the role of ICT is described as follows.

*An important means of enhancing learning and teaching across all three components is through the effective use of information and communications technologies.*

It then goes on to give some examples of ICT strands in relation to environmental studies.

In *Modern Languages: 5–14 National Guidelines*, Section 5 is devoted to detailed advice on the contribution of ICT, while the seven strands of *ICT 5–14* are viewed as:

> … *relevant to activities in the modern languages classroom, those of most immediate relevance include:*

Pupils in P5/6, involved in a European Partner schools project, gathered information on weather and climate in their own country and exchanged the data by e-mail with their European Partner school. The information received in both schools was entered in a database and compared with their own national information.

**Curriculum areas:**
environmental studies, mathematics

**ICT strands:**
*collecting and analysing information*, *communicating and collaborating*

- *creating and presenting: in publishing documents, project work or web pages*
- *searching and researching: in using search engines to find information on websites and in comparing information received*
- *communicating and collaborating: in composing and preparing individual and group communications through e-mail.*

ICT is described as a cross-curricular aspect in *The Structure and Balance of the Curriculum: 5–14 National Guidelines* and its importance stressed. Advice is given on the need for sufficient time to develop ICT skills and to use these effectively across the whole curriculum in primary schools. Secondary schools are encouraged to make arrangements within the flexibility factor to ensure provision for the development of ICT as a core skill.

A class of P3–P4 pupils worked in groups to engage in one of the following investigative tasks. In their work they tackled a number of the strands of ICT. They searched, collected and presented suitable information about:

- the local community to e-mail to pupils in another school in Scotland
- selected aspects of life in Scotland to e-mail to pupils (pen-pals) in another country
- the school to publish on a school website that was being set up.

In several 5–14 curriculum areas national guidelines dating from the early 1990s remain current. However, the advances in technology offer teachers and pupils new opportunities. For example, many schools have developed creative and innovative responses to the graphics potential of ICT in the programmes of study for art and design in *Expressive Arts 5–14* (SOED, 1992).

Further examples of ICT across the 5–14 curriculum, including in English language and in mathematics, are given in the *Guide for Teachers and Managers*.

Different groups of pupils chose from the above, searched and collected information from interviews, the library, teletext, CDs and the internet, and created and presented the information for the task selected using a desktop publishing package.

It is anticipated that, over time, schools will require further support in demonstrating ICT across 5–14 to assist implementation of these guidelines.

**Curriculum areas:**
English language, environmental studies

**ICT strands:**
*using the technology, creating and presenting, collecting and analysing, searching and researching, communicating and collaborating*

In S2, a group of pupils in two of the school's departments, Art and Design, Food Technology and Textiles, worked collaboratively to design and produce a suitable logo for embroidering on to a fishing club tie or handkerchief. They drew their first ideas on paper, then agreed and selected the most appropriate – a design featuring a fish. The design was drawn out in detail on paper and then scanned into a computer; the image was enhanced using a maximum number of colours and the computer linked to a Practical Operated Embroidery Machine (POEM) to produce the design using coloured threads.

**Contributing departments:**
Art and Design, Food Technology and Textiles

**ICT strand:**
*controlling and modelling*

In the World War II project described above, a group, working in mathematics activities, simulated a destroyer on a search-and-rescue mission. They worked out directions for a floor turtle (the destroyer) to search the possible locations of the rescue. They used a floor map using commands such as *forward 3, right 90, forward 3, left 90*. The starting point and these directions were given to a second group to follow to try to locate the site of the rescue.

**Curriculum area:**
mathematics

**ICT strand:**
*controlling and modelling*

Pupils in P7 engaged in the same international project, exchanged written information about themselves by e-mail, with photographs and drawings as attachments. They also had the opportunity to communicate with their partner school by videoconference and to use English, French and German.

**Curriculum areas:**
English language, modern languages

**ICT strand:**
*communicating and collaborating*

A historical study in a small rural primary school focused on local evidence of an early people, the Picts, living in the community. The pupils' investigations were enriched by using ICT to videoconference to the national museum to access a curator who demonstrated Pictish artefacts from the national collection, provided additional information on the lifestyle of the Picts and answered questions the pupils had prepared from their local research.

**Curriculum area:**
environmental studies

**ICT strands:**
*using the technology, communicating and collaborating*

In S1, in English and working at level C–E, a class was invited to consider the increasing impact of ICT on society with the aim of conducting a class debate highlighting positive and negative issues. They first viewed a video that introduced them to various examples. After researching the topic further and preparing written reports, pupils were grouped together based on whether they wished to opt for the side of the debate that would stress positive or negative findings.

**Curriculum area:**
English language

**ICT strands:**
*searching and researching, developing informed attitudes*

Pupils in P7 involved in a topic 'Journeys' searched the internet for travel information about place, people, mode and times of transport.

**Curriculum area:**
environmental studies

**ICT strand:**
*searching and researching*

Pupils engaged in a project 'World in the News' accessed the internet to view and read various newspapers preselected and bookmarked by the teacher, to compare their styles of reporting.

**Curriculum area:**
English language (for bias/genre)

**ICT strand:**
*searching and researching*

Section 7

# Specific Issues

## 7.1 ICT 5–14 and the relationship to other stages of learning

The 5–14 stages will make a significant contribution to the development in pupils of knowledge, skills and attitudes in ICT. However, ICT developed during these stages should be regarded as part of a longer-term development of an important core skill. This starts during the pre-school stage and continues through the remaining secondary school years, with ongoing progression through further/higher education, the world of work and in adult life. ICT experiences in 5–14 should be regarded as making a key contribution to the development of important lifelong learning skills.

ICT is not always specified as a compulsory content element of the curriculum at each stage or in each school subject. However, there is little doubt that it is regarded as making, at each stage, a significant contribution to general skills development, and ICT skills are now regarded as one of a set of core skills that is seen as vital to the educational development of young people.

## 7.2 ICT experiences in the early years

Even before they arrive in a pre-school centre many children will have had experience of the uses of ICT within their own home and in the wider community. Computers and ICT are now a significant part of their everyday lives, and within the pre-school centre children will often be provided with a range of opportunities to explore these technologies through role-play and first-hand experience.

While ICT can enhance children's learning across all aspects of development and learning, outlined in *A Curriculum Framework for Children 3 to 5* (Scottish CCC, 1999), children usually play with computers in pairs or in groups and this provides an important context for their emotional, personal and social development.

For the adults in pre-school centres ICT offers a new way of enhancing their own professional development, sharing ideas with others across the sector and making planning, recording and reporting more effective and efficient.

## 7.3 ICT provision beyond S2

Pupils will increasingly use ICT knowledge and skills within the subjects they have chosen beyond S2. This will consolidate and continue to develop their ICT capability. The articulation of ICT 5–14 with particular standard grade subjects is not straightforward because:

* there has been considerable change in technology since standard grade was introduced
* advances in the user interface and computer software mean that ICT learning outcomes can be achieved at an earlier stage
* not all pupils will select subjects with embedded ICT content.

Information technology is one of the framework of core skills developed under the Higher Still programme (for more information, see *Core Skills: Information for Senior Managers*, HSDU, 1999) and that now form part of the National Qualifications framework. This core skill focuses on 'the ability to use information technology to process information'. The core skill *information technology* is about students being able to:

- use computers to which they have access
- run and use software applications
- search for and retrieve information.

The strands in ICT 5–14 articulate well with these outcomes and progression from ICT 5–14 to the Higher Still core skill will be appropriate, coherent and apply to all pupils. Specific 5–14 levels and core skill levels will continue to evolve in the future.

The place of IT as a core skill within the Higher Still framework moves some way towards the proposal that by 2002 most school leavers should have a good understanding of ICT (*Connecting the Learning Society*, DfEE, 1997). The core skill in itself is not designed to produce IT specialists and there are specific courses available to enable students to develop this role.

## 7.4 ICT outwith school

There is little doubt that ICT will play an increasing role in the lives of young people outside school. The impact on the home and on leisure activities will be significant. Pupils will increasingly access ICT at home and in less formal educational settings such out-of-school clubs, drop-in centres and cybercafés. The school curriculum must recognise this, while acknowledging varying levels of access and experience, and draw examples from areas that are familiar and motivating to pupils. ICT also has a role in developing a coherent framework of concepts that allows pupils to understand the impact ICT is making on the world and to ensure that all pupils develop the skills they need to be successful in an ICT-rich environment.

## 7.5 Relationship with other national ICT initiatives

It is important to see ICT 5–14 in the context of a coherent, dynamic strategy to enhance the use of ICT in Scottish schools. This strategy is addressing recognised issues to promote progress through the provision of resources such as hardware, software and connectivity; training and staff development opportunities; and online curriculum support. National initiatives relevant to this strategy include the following.

- The National Grid for Learning (NGfL) Scotland
  By 2002, all schools will be connected to the National Grid for Learning (NGfL) and the programme includes national targets for the ratio of pupils to computers. The grid aims to raise achievement, promote social inclusion, widen participation in learning and provide professional advice and support. Its content and infrastructure will allow schools to access the most up-to-date resources, and to disseminate good practice by communicating electronically with colleagues. While the NGfL is a UK-wide programme and one that extends beyond schools, NGfL Scotland (www.ngflscotland.gov.uk) is developing to meet distinctive Scottish needs.

- Scottish Virtual Teachers' Centre (SVTC)
  The SVTC is the part of the National Grid for Learning designed specifically for schools. It supports teachers and school librarians in the effective use of the internet. It provides a forum for educational professionals to meet, exchange ideas and disseminate good practice. Services developing on the SVTC are based around a website (www.svtc.org.uk) and include links, materials, discussion areas and electronic mail lists.

- The New Opportunities Fund (NOF) training

  The NOF has provided resources to train all teachers and librarians in the effective use of ICT in schools. It is a three-year programme, running to 2002. Training is based on the development of ICT skills and confidence in the use of ICT throughout the curriculum and in areas of professional practice.

In addition a number of other training and staff development opportunities are available. New requirements now in place in pre-service training for teachers mean that all teachers entering service will have attained an agreed level of competence in their ICT skills.

Further information on these, and other current developments, is available online in the Scottish Virtual Teachers' Centre (SVTC) (www.svtc.org.uk) and the National Grid for Learning Scotland (www.ngflscotland.gov.uk).